DO THE WORK!
AFFORDABLE AND CLEAN ENERGY

COMMITTING TO THE UN'S SUSTAINABLE DEVELOPMENT GOALS

JULIE KNUTSON

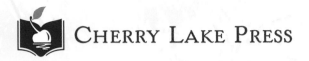

CHERRY LAKE PRESS

Published in the United States of America by Cherry Lake Publishing Group
Ann Arbor, Michigan
www.cherrylakepublishing.com

Reading Adviser: Beth Walker Gambro, MS, Ed., Reading Consultant, Yorkville, IL

Photo Credits: © Gencho Petkov/Shutterstock.com, cover, 1; © Melada photo/Shutterstock.com, 5;
Infographic From The Sustainable Development Goals Report 2021, by United Nations Department of Economic
and Social Affairs © 2021 United Nations. Reprinted with the permission of the United Nations, 7; © beerkoff/
Shutterstock.com, 8; © Vasyl Yosypchuk/Shutterstock.com, 9; © DGLimages/Shutterstock.com, 10; © Keith
Bell/Shutterstock.com, 13; © AS photostudio/Shutterstock.com, 14; © Rawpixel.com/Shutterstock.com, 17;
© GLRL/Shutterstock.com, 18; © Ultrakwang/Shutterstock.com, 21; © Juice Verve/Shutterstock.com, 22;
© T.W. van Urk/Shutterstock.com, 25; © Marcus Wennrich/Shutterstock.com, 26; © Olivier Le Moal/
Shutterstock.com, 28

Cherry Lake Press is an imprint of Cherry Lake Publishing Group.

Library of Congress Cataloging-in-Publication Data
Names: Knutson, Julie, author.
Title: Do the work! : affordable and clean energy / by Julie Knutson.
Description: Ann Arbor, Michigan : Cherry Lake Publishing, [2022] | Series: Committing to the UN's sustainable
    development goals | Includes bibliographical references. | Audience: Grades 2-3
Identifiers: LCCN 2022005355 | ISBN 9781668909232 (hardcover) | ISBN 9781668910832 (paperback) |
    ISBN 9781668914014 (pdf) | ISBN 9781668912423 (ebook)
Subjects: LCSH: Clean energy industries—Juvenile literature. | Renewable energy sources—Juvenile literature. |
    Sustainable development—Juvenile literature.
Classification: LCC HD9502.5.C542 K596 2022 | DDC 333.79/4—dc23/eng/20220208
LC record available at https://lccn.loc.gov/2022005355

Cherry Lake Publishing Group would like to acknowledge the work of the Partnership for 21st Century
Learning, a Network of Battelle for Kids. Please visit http://www.battelleforkids.org/networks/p21
for more information.

Printed in the United States of America
Corporate Graphics

The content of this publication has not been approved by the United Nations and does not reflect the views of the
United Nations or its officials or Member States. For more information on the Sustainable Development Goals,
please visit https://www.un.org/sustainabledevelopment.

ABOUT THE AUTHOR

Julie Knutson is an author-educator who writes extensively about global citizenship and the
Sustainable Development Goals. Her previous book, *Global Citizenship: Engage in the Politics
of a Changing World* (Nomad Press, 2020), introduces key concepts about 21st-century
interconnectedness to middle grade and high school readers. She hopes that this series will
inspire young readers to take action and embrace their roles as changemakers in the world.

TABLE OF CONTENTS

CHAPTER 1

Meet the SDGs

With the flip of a switch or the push of a button, what can light up a dark room? What keeps the food in your freezer cold, while also letting you heat up leftovers in the microwave? What allows laptops, iPads, and cell phones to charge and function?

That's right . . . it's electricity, the force that keeps life as many of us know it humming.

If you live in the United States, there's about a 60 percent chance that your everyday electricity consumption is powered by **fossil fuels**. This is a problem. Why? Because those energy sources—like coal, oil, and natural gas—are nonrenewable, meaning their supply is limited. Burning fossil fuels also produces **carbon emissions** that contribute to **climate change**.

When you think of electricity, the name Thomas Edison might come to mind. In addition to creating new kinds of telegraphs and the phonograph, he is also credited with inventing the electric lightbulb in 1879.

STOP AND THINK: *How do you use electricity in your everyday life? Spend a day tracking your electricity use, from making your morning toast to taking your evening shower. How would your life be different without this convenience?*

Across the world, people are working to develop new, clean energy solutions. Scientists, policy experts, and engineers are also working to bring electricity to the estimated 770 million people in the world who are not connected to an electricity **grid**. These clean energy **advocates** are all united by a common goal—to achieve a world that ensures "access to affordable, reliable, **sustainable** and modern energy for all." You can join them! Read on to learn how you can help make the **United Nations**' (UN) seventh Sustainable Development Goal (SDG), "Affordable and Clean Energy," a reality.

What Are the SDGs?

The UN announced the 17 SDGs in 2015. These global goals range from "No Poverty" (SDG 1) to "Quality Education" (SDG 4) to "Climate Action" (SDG 13). At the core, the SDGs are about making life better now and in the future for "people and the planet." All 193 UN member states have agreed to cooperate in reaching the 169 SDG targets by 2030.

"Affordable & Clean Energy" is the seventh goal on the list. The aim of SDG 7 is to provide universal access to clean, modern energy. This means that all health care facilities and schools will get electricity. People will have new opportunities to live safer, healthier lives.

ONE THIRD
OF THE WORLD'S POPULATION USE
DANGEROUS AND INEFFICIENT COOKING SYSTEMS [2019]

2.6 BILLION PEOPLE

759 MILLION PEOPLE

LACK ACCESS
TO ELECTRICITY

3 OUT OF **4**
OF THEM LIVE IN
SUB-SAHARAN AFRICA
[2019]

ENERGY EFFICIENCY IMPROVEMENT RATE
NEEDS ACCELERATION

ANNUAL EFFICIENCY IMPROVEMENT RATE

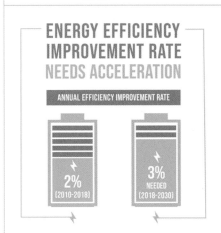

2%
[2010-2018]

3%
NEEDED
[2018-2030]

ACCELERATED ACTION ON MODERN RENEWABLE ENERGY IS NEEDED — ESPECIALLY IN HEATING AND TRANSPORT SECTORS

MODERN RENEWABLE SHARE OF TOTAL FINAL ENERGY CONSUMPTION [2018]

 ELECTRICITY SECTOR
25.4%

 HEAT SECTOR
9.2%

 TRANSPORT SECTOR
3.4%

THE SUSTAINABLE DEVELOPMENT GOALS REPORT 2021: UNSTATS.UN.ORG/SDGS/REPORT/2021/

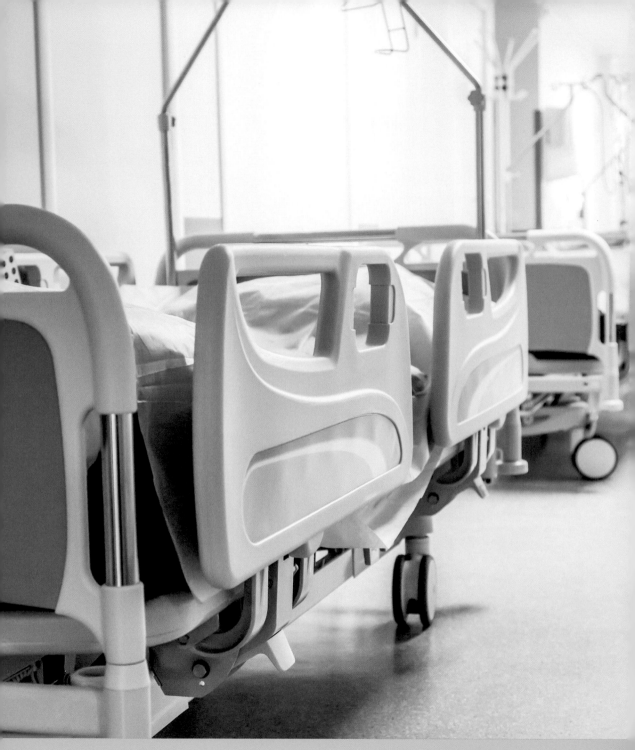

Currently, one in four health facilities in low-income countries lacks electricity.

According to Conservation International, the average person generates about 5 tons of carbon dioxide a year. That is roughly the same as burning 5,335 pounds (2,420 kilograms) of coal.

Related Goals

In today's world, there are still children who collect firewood with which to cook and to heat their homes with instead of going to school. There are millions of people who inhale unhealthy amounts of indoor air pollution produced by **kerosene** and other heating oils. There are landscapes polluted by mining for coal, oil, and natural gas.

Everyday activities like running the dishwasher increase your carbon footprint.

Through these examples, it's easy to see that SDG 7 intersects with other goals such as "Quality Education," "Good Health and Well-Being," and "Climate Action." The 17 SDGs do not exist alone. Action on one helps drive change in other areas. Working to create a world with affordable and clean energy is critical to a more just and sustainable future for all people.

What's a Carbon Footprint?

Your carbon footprint is the measure of **greenhouse gas emissions** that your activities produce in a year. According to the Nature Conservancy, the average carbon footprint for a U.S. resident is about 17 tons. Globally, the average is about 4 tons. Reducing our individual and collective footprints is critical. As the Nature Conservancy notes, "To have the best chance of avoiding a [3.6 degrees Fahrenheit (2 degrees Celsius)] rise in global temperatures, the average global carbon footprint per year needs to drop under 2 tons by 2050." Throughout this book, you'll learn about actions that you, your family, and classmates can take to tread more lightly.

CHAPTER 2

Why Do We Have Goals?

Imagine that you want to learn how to do something new. Maybe it's riding a skateboard, writing your own comic, or learning the capitals of every state. By choosing or coming up with something, you've set a goal! But . . . where do you start? What's the process for achieving it?

After setting a goal, a person typically maps out a path for achieving it, noting the different steps that it will take from start to finish. Goals should be "SMART," or Specific, Measurable, Achievable, Relevant, and Timed. Your goals should be within reach in a given amount of time.

STOP AND THINK: *What goals do you have? What timeline could you set for achieving them, and what steps could you take to reach them?*

Hydroelectric power is captured from the kinetic energy of falling water. The energy produced by flowing water circulates through turbines, which convert it into mechanical energy.

The expansion of solar energy helps create jobs.

Large organizations set goals too. And just as a person might set benchmarks for achieving a goal, so do groups. Each of the UN's 17 SDGs has specific targets and **indicators**. These targets are steps that must be met to ensure progress of the larger goal. The indicators are a way of measuring success.

Progress on SDG 7 is measured by the following targets and indicators:

- Universal access to affordable, modern energy services by 2030. This will be measured by the percentage of people with access to electricity and the percentage of people who use clean fuel as an energy source.

- Increase **renewable energy** sources, like wind and solar power. Success will be measured by the total percentage of consumed energy that comes from renewable sources.
- By 2030, double the global rate of energy **efficiency**.
- Enhance international cooperation in developing and generating clean energy technology.
- By 2030, expand **infrastructure** so all people worldwide can enjoy clean and reliable energy.

The First Country Powered by Renewable Energy?

The mountainous country of Nepal sits high in the Himalayan range. Its rugged landscape has historically made developing an electricity grid very difficult. But with support from neighbors China, India, and Bangladesh, Nepal is harnessing a powerful source of renewable energy—water that flows from the country's mountains into rivers. As author Kayla Stansbury explains in a 2019 article from *Faces* magazine, Nepal's rivers give it "the potential to produce 90,000 megawatts of **hydroelectric energy**, which is enough for the whole country and then some." This project involves building 12 hydroelectric plants that will provide renewable energy not only to Nepal, but also to China, India, and Bangladesh. The project shows how "enhanced international cooperation" can help build a more energy-secure and sustainable future.

Do the Work! Contribute to the Goals at Home

Maybe it's unplugging electronics that are not in use, or encouraging your family to line-dry clothes rather than loading them in the dryer. Or maybe it is reminding your family members to turn down the thermostat when they're not home. There are so many things that you can do at home to act on SDG 7! Read on to learn more.

- **Reduce Use** — Reset your energy use habits. Turn off lights when you leave a room. Take shorter showers and unplug electronics like toasters, TVs, and computers when not in use. When boiling water, cover pots with lids, which can reduce the amount of energy used by up to 75 percent!

To save energy at home, encourage your family members to recycle unwanted items, use cold water in the washing machine, and unplug unused electronics.

- **Educate Yourself and Others** — Ask questions about why the world needs renewable and clean energy. Read about available energy sources and their pros and cons. Learn about electricity and how it works. Educate yourself and others about solar, wind, and hydroelectric power. Read about changemakers like William Kamkwamba, the engineer-author of *The Boy Who Harnessed the Wind*, to learn what inspired them to try to find solutions to global energy challenges.

Encourage your parents to switch to energy-efficient lightbulbs.

- **Contribute to Household Decisions** — It doesn't have to be something as major as convincing your parents to install solar panels on your house. Simple changes like replacing lightbulbs can have a major impact too. The U.S. Department of Energy notes that **light-emitting diode** (LED) lights "use only 20 percent to 25 percent of the energy and last 15 to 25 times longer than the traditional **incandescent bulbs** they replace." Encourage the people with the buying power in your house to make the switch to save energy.

With a family member, you can also take an online carbon footprint quiz. The Nature Conservancy's website offers a series of questions to calculate your household's yearly carbon emissions. It also offers solutions and strategies for reducing your carbon footprint.

Do the Work! Contribute to the Goals at School

You can use many of the ideas for reducing energy at home at school too! Educate your teachers, classmates, and school leaders on why clean energy matters and how your school can reduce its carbon footprint.

- **Educate** — Have you ever seen a school at night with all the lights on? At school, remind teachers to switch off lights when people are out of the classroom at lunch or recess. Also, encourage your school leaders to set motion sensor controls that turn off lights automatically when no one is in a room.

Consider planting trees at school to offset carbon emissions!
You can host an annual tree planting event each April on Arbor Day.

Your science teacher may have some ideas for sustainable projects you can create.

- **Start a Club** — Launch a sustainability club at your school! You can set up classroom recycling bins, launch a school composting program, and host Earth Day or Energy Awareness Month events. You can also read books and invite guest speakers who work to provide the world with clean and affordable energy.

  STOP AND THINK: *What else could you do to promote awareness of clean and renewable energy at your school?*

- **Fundraise** — Through organizations like Green School Alliance, you and your classmates can sell kits for growing small trees. The kits include a biodegradable cup and lid, growing pellet, tree seed, and growing instructions. Organizations like One Tree Planted also offer fundraising opportunities. In 2020, first- through fifth-grade students in Berkeley Unified School District raised more than $6,000 to plant trees in areas of California that were devastated by wildfires.

Extreme weather makes events like the 2021 power outages in Texas more likely to occur. Coastal areas are especially at risk.

The United States is divided into three electrical grids. One covers the East Coast, another covers the West, and the third covers Texas. The decision for Texas to have a separate grid was made more than 100 years ago because state officials didn't want to have to follow **federal** cost and safety **regulations**. So while neighboring states like Oklahoma also experienced the storm, they didn't suffer the same effects. They were connected to power sources in places such as Kansas and Missouri that didn't bear the brunt of the wintery weather.

That's not to say that this is a problem that could only happen in Texas. The U.S. electrical grid is aging. Much of it was built 60 to 70 years ago. According to the American Society of Civil Engineers, it was built to last 50 years. In Texas and elsewhere, the electrical infrastructure hasn't been updated to form more **resilient** communities.

You can encourage decision-makers in your community and across the world to build more efficient and reliable energy systems by taking the following action:

Write to your elected officials. Tell them to support policies and programs that promote clean, affordable, and reliable energy infrastructure. Ask them to update energy grids and offer **incentives** *for using energy-efficient appliances and renewable energy such as solar and wind power. Also encourage them to make "greener" and healthier communities by building bike and walking paths and transit systems to reduce reliance on vehicles powered by fossil fuels.*

INDEX